TOWER HAMLET

KT-519-824

C001279323

Say
Good-bye

An Anthology by
New Writers in Prison

New Writers' Voices
Readers House

Literacy Volunteers of New York City

NEW WRITERS' VOICES ™ was made possible by grants from: an anonymous foundation; Exxon Corporation; Scripps Howard Foundation; Philip Morris Companies, Inc.; Garry Trudeau and Penguin USA; and H. W. Wilson Foundation.

ATTENTION READERS: We would like to hear what you think about our books. Please send your comments or suggestions to:

The Editors
Literacy Volunteers of New York City
121 Avenue of the Americas
New York, NY 10013

Copyright © 1993 by Readers House, the publishing division of Literacy Volunteers of New York City Inc.

All rights reserved. This book may not be reproduced in whole or in part, in any form or by any means, without permission.

Printed in the United States of America.

98 97 96 95 94 93 10 9 8 7 6 5 4 3 2 1

First LVNYC Printing: April 1993

ISBN 1-56853-005-6

New Writers' Voices is a series of books published by Literacy Volunteers of New York City Inc., 121 Avenue of the Americas, New York, NY 10013. The words, "New Writers' Voices," are a trademark of Readers House/ Literacy Volunteers of New York City. READERS HOUSE and colophon are trademarks of Literacy Volunteers of New York City.

Cover designed by Paul Davis Studio; interior designed by Jules Perlmutter.

The articles in this book were edited with the cooperation and consent of the authors. Every effort has been made to locate the copyright owners of material reproduced in this book. Omissions brought to our attention will be corrected in subsequent editions.

Executive Director, LVNYC: Lilliam Barrios-Paoli
Publishing Director, LVNYC: Nancy McCord
Managing Editor: Sarah Kirshner
Publishing Coordinator: Yvette Martinez-Gonzalez
Marketing/Production Manager: Elizabeth Bluemle
LVNYC is an affiliate of Literacy Volunteers of America

Acknowledgments

*L*iteracy Volunteers of New York City gratefully acknowledges the generous support of the following foundations and corporations that made the publication of READERS HOUSE books possible: an anonymous foundation; Exxon Corporation; Scripps Howard Foundation; Philip Morris Companies, Inc.; Garry Trudeau and Penguin USA; and H. W. Wilson Foundation.

We deeply appreciate the contributions of the following suppliers: an anonymous donor (cover stock); Arcata Graphics Company (cover and text printing and binding); Boise Cascade Corporation (text stock); Cam Steel Rule Die Works Inc. (steel cutting die for display); ComCom Inc. (text typesetting); Delta Corrugated Container (corrugated display); MCUSA (display header); Phototype Color Graphics (cover color separations).

For their guidance, support and hard work, we are indebted to the LVNYC Board of Directors' Publishing Committee: James E. Galton, Marvel Comics Ltd.; Virginia Barber, Virginia Barber Literary Agency, Inc.; Doris Bass, Scholastic, Inc.; Jeff Brown; Jerry Butler; George P. Davidson, Ballantine Books; Joy M. Gannon, St. Martin's Press; Walter Kiechel, *Fortune*; Geraldine E. Rhoads; Virginia Rice, Reader's Digest; Martin Singerman, News America Publishing, Inc.; James L. Stanko, James Money Management, Inc.; Arnold Schaab and F. Robert Stein of Pryor, Cashman, Sherman & Flynn.

Thanks also to George Davidson, Caron Harris and Steve Palmer of Ballantine Books for producing this book; Lisa Holzer for her thoughtful copyediting and suggestions; to Candace Wainwright for proofreading; and to Allegra D'Adamo and Pam Johnson for their dedicated work on this project.

We would like to thank the following people and institutions for their assistance with this project: CALIFORNIA: Mary Lou Browning, Contra Costa County Jail School Program; Linda White; ILLINOIS: Lois Barr, Joliet Correctional Center; Clyde A. Winters, PACE Institute, Cook County Jail; MASSACHUSETTS: Eugene Gramarosa, Hampden County Correctional Facility; Pat Mew, Hampshire County House of Correction; MICHIGAN: Judith Nash, Standish Maximum Correctional Facility; Don Swajanen, Alger Correctional Facility; NEW YORK: Evelyn H. Murov, Hudsonview School, Sing-Sing Correctional Facility; NEW MEXICO: Dale Marlin; Cynthia Sanchez, Western New Mexico Correctional Facility; Carol Sayre, New Mexico Women's Correctional Facility; OKLAHOMA: Ed Stolz, Oklahoma Department of Corrections; Jan Benson and Robert J. Jarrett, Lexington Assessment and Reception Center; Judy Wells, Mack H. Alford Correctional Center; SOUTH CAROLINA: Kathy Freeman, South Carolina Department of Corrections; VIRGINIA: Dana Rhodenizer, Staunton Correctional Center; WISCONSIN: Carol Gabler, LVA-Chippewa Valley, Eau Claire.

For their hard work and enthusiastic participation, we would like to thank our student authors.

Our thanks to Paul Davis Studio and Myrna Davis, Paul Davis, Lisa Mazur, Hajime Ando, Haruetai Muodtong and Chalkley Calderwood for their inspired design of the covers of these books. Thanks also to Jules Perlmutter for his sensitive design of the interior of this book.

Tower Hamlets	
Suppliers Code	AVA
Price	£2.95
Invoice Date	01/11/2006
LOC	BOW
Class	428.6
Barcode	C001279323

Contents

Never Say Good-bye

David Patrick McKee, *Massachusetts*

When I was 26 years old, I lost the two closest people in my life, first my wife and then my son. I loved them more than anyone in the world.

One day, I received a phone call from the hospital where my son was. They said he was getting worse. I went straight there. My son got weaker and weaker. I couldn't stop crying. I hurt so deep inside. I asked my son to please hang in there and not leave me. My son said, "Dad, never say good-bye." I always said that to him when he was growing up.

My son knew he was going to die, but he also knew he was going to heaven. Before he died, he said, "Hello, Dad, I'll see you again in heaven." And I said, "Hello, son, I'll see you in heaven. I love you very, very much and always will."

"Please, Dad, keep me in your heart," he said. And I said, "Son, keep me in your heart each and every day."

My son died right after I said that. I began to cry and asked God and his son, Jesus, to take care of my wife and son until I got to heaven. I will never say good-bye.

Advice to New Writers

From the creative writing class at
Hampshire House of Correction,
Northampton, Massachusetts

I was afraid that I didn't have any talent for writing
or that I couldn't possibly do it. But I learned that yes,
I could do it and that the more I wrote, the easier it
became. A few things that helped me overcome my
doubts were 1) to write for myself, 2) to let people
help me, and 3) the most important one, to go with
it and just have fun.

Michael Champagne

My fear has always been about reading what I write,
not the criticism but just reading it. I have met a lot
of new writers and each time I do, I learn many new
ways to do things.

Ronald James Kelley

Don't be afraid to share your pieces with the class; it
will help you considerably. Listen up and take any
criticism in a positive way. That will also help you.
Relax and open up; it helps.

Mark H.

Do I Have to Let Go?

Anonymous, *California*

There is no one in this world I love
As much as I love you.
There's no one else can make me do
The things I'd do for you.

And now it seems I've hurt your heart.
You do not want me close.
Now I fear you'll never see
It's you I want the most.

You say I've shown you no respect.
You say I've hurt you deep.
And every time I talk with you,
I always make you weep.

It's true that I have been real bad.
I've run around this place.
But when I close my eyes at night,
I always see your face.

I hate to keep on hurting you
Because I love you so,
But maybe I don't know how to love.
Should I just let you go?

Living

William G. Owen, *California*

I remember the fragrant smell of the open fields with patches of multicolored flowers in bloom, each one nodding its head in recognition of me, for I've passed this way before.

I remember a little country schoolhouse with a pond nearby teeming with frogs, turtles and crawdads—the teacher's nightmare but, to an adventurous child, a delight.

I remember a walk in the woods every Saturday with a .410 shotgun or a .22 rifle. I'd leave the house at eight in the morning and be home in time for supper and only have tired feet.

I remember when a dime could buy you a ride on a bus or a ticket to the show, a hamburger or a comic book or two Cokes. The carnival was free and the rides cost only one thin dime.

I remember the Depression when my dad worked for the W.P.A. and earned ten dollars a week. We were able to pay rent plus utilities, buy a week's supply of groceries and still have enough left for a movie.

I remember the war years and the president's

fireside chats. The whole family would gather around the radio and listen to the news or Joe Louis winning another fight or a soap opera.

I remember patriotic parades, bands playing in the park and politicians making speeches while people threw streamers out of tall buildings, celebrating the war's end.

I remember a loving family that taught me Christian values, but gave me spankings when I needed them (which was quite often). But always with the words, "Son, this is going to hurt me more than it does you."

I remember always going to church on Sunday mornings. But I didn't mind because I got to be with my friends whose parents also made them go to church.

I remember a most joyful and loving and learning time with adventures and misadventures. It's something I will have always—the memories of childhood.

I Wonder

Anonymous, *California*

I wonder what I was before.
Did I ever fight a war?
Was I a powerful and noble king
Or just a countess's weekly fling?
Did I pick cotton in the fields all day
Or just sit and idle my time away?
Did I ever mine for gold
Or get lost and frozen in the cold?

All this I wonder about me,
Yet my rank is not important
As long as I was free.

Family Reunion

Zhang Wen, *New York*

When I was a child, our family visited my grandparents in the Fuchou mountains in China. We lived in the city and made the trip to the mountains with my aunts and cousins and other close family friends. We went in March to celebrate a holiday that is like the American Thanksgiving Day.

It was a very long climb to reach my grandparents' home. It was easy for me because my parents carried me.

Now that I am older, I think about the trips we made. The trail was steep, rocky and hot. Sometimes we stopped for water or something to eat. It's hard to believe we returned year after year to begin the trip again. After two or three hours of hard climbing, someone would yell "We're there" or "They're here," depending on who saw whom first.

It's unbelievable how quickly we forgot about the heat, the sweat and the long climb. Our tired, soaked bodies were refreshed with hugs, kisses and love. I also remember the foods we ate: chicken, fish, lobster, crabs, clams, shrimp and a sweet bread that I loved.

Cell Bound Number Two

Donall Eubanks-El, *Michigan*

*T*rapped once again in the dismal crypts.
It's like running in a gun fight without any clips.
Or being chased into a dead-end street
With your back against the wall as you face
    defeat.

It seemed you were one of the lucky ones,
Strong and unwilling to fall,
But now it looks like you've forgotten
The lessons you were taught after all.

You said it would be different
If you were given one more chance.
So life played your song,
But you refused to dance.

Now you're back among the forgotten,
Broke and in blue.
You should have learned your lesson the first time
But now you're Cell Bound Number Two.

Living in New Mexico

Diane Chavez, *New Mexico*

New Mexico is known as The Land of Enchantment. For me, it has been The Land of Entrapment.

Speaking as a Hispanic person, we have a very high poverty rate, poor education and low-paying jobs. Rich white people have taken over our land. We, the Hispanic people, can barely afford to pay rent, much less own houses of our own. The Hispanic people have been pushed out.

Because I am poor and Hispanic, I did not have a good education so that I could get a high-paying job. This is one reason that I led a life of crime and drugs in New Mexico.

My life put me in a prison where there is no help for the common junkie. I feel that if the government of New Mexico put more money into rehab programs and education, New Mexico would no longer be The Land of Entrapment but The Land of Enchantment, The Land of the Free.

Love

Anonymous, *California*

*F*alling in love is like getting hit by a large truck and yet not being mortally wounded. Just sick to your stomach, high one minute, low the next. Hot, cold, forever horny, full of hope and enthusiasm with momentary depressions that wipe you out.

It is also not being able to remove the smile from your face, loving life with a mad passionate intensity and feeling ten years younger.

Love appears with no warning signals. You fall into it as if pushed from a high diving board. No time to think about what's happening. It's inevitable. An event you can't control. A crazy, heart-stopping, roller coaster ride that just has to take its course.

Neither person expected it. Oh sure, they were attracted to each other, the whole sexual bit was in full swing. But love?

Doing Time

Charles Ham, *New York*

Sitting in a cell,
Feeling like a caged animal straight out of hell.
Feeling so bad for being here,
Knowing that I cannot help my family
    with tender loving care.
Nor can I lend them a hand.
Feeling very uncomfortable about that
    because I'm supposed to be a man.
But even though I'm doing time,
I'm trying to do something with my mind.
Before I could hardly read or write,
But now I can do a little of both.
Maybe, in the future,
    I'll be reunited with my family and friends.
Until then,
Here I sit in a cell,
Caged like an animal straight out of hell.
Doing time
But not letting time do me.

My Name

Sherri Baker, *California*

Sitting here,
Hating
Every minute,
Relief from my
Racing mind
Is nowhere in sight.

Beyond a shadow of
A doubt, I
Know I can't
Even begin to count the
Reasons why I can't seem to stay free.

The Importance of My Family

Warm, loving, caring, sharing, dedicated, devoted, emotional—these words describe a fraction of what my family means to me.

Due to irresponsible judgment, I have temporarily lost my freedom. And most of all, I have lost time—time that I could have spent holding, loving and caring for my children and fiancée. It is easy to say "I love you" and "I care about you." However, it means the world to be able to show your emotions physically, to share the happy moments as well as the sad ones with the people you love, your family.

The time that I am away can never be replaced. Cherish every waking hour of the day that you have to spend with your family.

A family is like the keys of a piano; each member sounds a different note. However, when joined together in harmony, beautiful music is made. And when a member of the family is gone, the family is out of tune.

Worth Repeating

Mr. Nakeem-X, *Michigan*

My name is Gossip. I have no respect for justice. I maim without killing. I break and ruin lives. I am cunning and malicious and gather strength with age. The more I am talked about, the more I am believed.

I flourish at every level of society. My victims are helpless. They cannot protect themselves against me because I have no face. To track me down is impossible. The harder you try, the more elusive I become. I am nobody's friend.

Once I tarnish a reputation, it is never the same. I topple governments and wreck marriages. I ruin careers and cause sleepless nights. I spawn suspicion and generate grief. Even my name hisses.

I am called Gossip—office gossip, party gossip. Gossip. I make headlines and heartaches. Before you repeat a story, ask yourself "Is it true? Is it necessary?" If not, shut up!

Personal Ad

Michael Brown, *Oklahoma*

I am a 1969 Camaro. I was customized in a small garage east of Oklahoma City just a year ago. I have a 427 hemi underneath my hood. Searching for a 427 Ford Fairlane.

The Little King

Ervin S. Knight, *Virginia*

When I was a little boy, I thought I was a king—king of all the wrong things. I became a shadow, slipping around at night, stealing other people's property. I thought I would never get caught. I thought I could do it forever.

One night, I stole much more than I could ever handle, thinking I was still a king. I got caught and sent to jail. The judge hit the hammer and said "No bail." Now I'm doing time in prison, catching pure hell.

Test

Anonymous, *Illinois*

❦

*T*oday we have a test.
This is the worst day.
I look at the questions very carefully.
My body begins to shake.
The pencil almost slips out of my hand,
But I will not lose.
I hold the pencil tight
And I'm ready to fight with the questions.
Huge drops of sweat come to my palm
And spread on the paper faintly.

Dorothy

Anonymous, *Virginia*

I met Dorothy at school when I was 14. She only stood about four feet, six inches tall and at first, I wasn't attracted to her. But after a couple of weeks, she caught my eye. She was only 13.

My mother died right after I started going with Dorothy. A few weeks later, my father abandoned us and then my older brother left. I had to quit school to care for my two young sisters.

I got a job at the sawmill to support us. I also got a job at the grocery store/service station at night. The owner of the sawmill sold me two acres of land with a one-room house. It cost $5.00, but it took me six months to save for it. I only made 35 cents an hour at the sawmill and 15 cents an hour at the service station.

I added four rooms to the house at no cost. I dug and poured the new foundation with my own hands. The owner of the sawmill gave me the lumber. His sons helped me build the addition.

While I was building the house, a farmer asked me to help run his farm. He had lost both his legs and his sons had just joined the army. I ran his farm and my sisters and I lived in our old homestead.

Dorothy got pregnant and we secretly got married. Dorothy stayed at home with her parents because I couldn't take on any more responsibilities. I visited her every other night and brought the baby milk. Dorothy stayed in school while her mother cared for the baby.

After a year and a half, I went to claim Dorothy as my wife. Her parents were mad until they found out I had my own house all paid for and was doing better than they were.

Dorothy, my baby daughter, my two sisters and I all moved to the house I had built. Dorothy and I were married for 23 years. We had three more children, all boys. But Dorothy and our fifth child died at its birth.

Inner Beauty

James C. Joyner, Jr., *California*

❧

I cannot see your face
But I feel your beauty inside,
Your sense of humor, your honesty
And your pride.
A person can be scarred on the outside
And the hurt may never mend
But the beauty that is hard to mar
Is the beauty that lies within.
I do not need to see you
To know if you are beautiful to see.
By reading all your letters,
Your beauty appears to me.
I cannot see your face
But I like what's inside.

Shine Boys

Vincent Younis, *New Mexico*

*S*aturday, kind of drunk. He was talking to all the *turistas* that walked past him. This one Tejano* stopped to ask him something and before you know it, he had struck up a full-fledged conversation with the gentleman.

The Tejano had on this nice, expensive cowboy hat with a turquoise and silver hatband. Yankee couldn't give him enough compliments on how nice it was. Finally Yankee asked if he could just put it on for a minute. The Tejano was reluctant at first, but then said all right.

Yankee was a Tejano-hater at heart. As soon as the man gave him the hat, he threw it down on the ground and started to stomp the shit out of it. Naturally the Tejano started to kick Yankee. And before anyone knew it, there was a mini-riot in front of the pool hall and the cops were carting Yankee and the Tejano off to jail.

*a man from Texas

I Love You

Leonard Daigneault, *Massachusetts*

Does it matter if I am old, paunchy, bald,
When I tell you I love you?
Within me lies and thrives great beauty
Longing to be expressed.
What better way to show it than to say
"I love you."
It may not be important to anyone but me.
What do I care!
Having been exposed to your personality,
I fell in love—crawled, stumbled, bumbled.
It was a slow process,
But I hope to know and love you more.
And that's it, Lady.

Jail Routine

Michael C., *Massachusetts*

From spring to late fall, the inmates are given an hour in the yard twice a day. In winter, we are kept inside so everyone gets claustrophobic.

During yard time, there is basketball, softball and weight lifting for inmate recreation. I never cared for any of that but prefer to have a brief taste of privacy. Walking around, breathing fresh air for a change, puts my mind at rest.

In the woods around the jail, there are hawks. My greatest prizes are hawk feathers I find in the yard. I bring each feather to my cell and add it to my collection. Many times, I stroke a feather and see in my mind a hawk flying free.

A Colt Named Midnight

Jerry L. Brennan, *Oklahoma*

I had a coal-black colt named Midnight. His mother was a bay thoroughbred named Lady Luck. Lady Luck died while she was giving birth.

I didn't know for sure how I was going to raise a colt. A friend had a cow that lost her calf and he let me have her. Getting her to take the colt was a job, but finally she did and raised him as her own. When the cow bedded down, the colt lay beside her. I don't think he knew if he was a horse or a cow.

Midnight grew into a real nice horse, about 14 hands high. He had no marks and looked like an Arabian. I trained him to do whatever I wanted— we worked cattle together. No one could ride him but me. Midnight was a horse anyone would like to have, but I wouldn't sell him for any amount of money.

Midnight died on June 15, 1985, when he was 20 years old. I buried him on my farm.

Dear Lost Feeling

M. Harris, *Virginia*

*D*ear Lost Feeling,

I understand now, Lost Feeling, that I do have a very loving and caring family. As I look back in time, I always had thoughts that I was alone and didn't belong in the family. I lived with these thoughts and their pain for many years.

In the last year, I have become very close to my family. My mother and my little sister came to visit me and I was very happy to see them. My mother said, "I love you, son." I hadn't heard those words in a long, long time.

If only I had not waited so damn long to tell my feelings. But now we are close. Maybe time will tell more about these lost feelings. What makes it so sad is that I feel much better expressing my feelings.

Love from Parts Unknown

Days of Drugs

Anonymous, *California*

❦

I remember
Days long ago,
Walking to school,
Fitting in with the guys.

I remember
Halloween in the fourth grade,
Smoking dope for the first time,
Fitting in with the guys.

I remember
Being young in L.A.,
Shooting reds and being cool,
Fitting in with the guys.

I remember
My youth and days gone by,
Fixing crank and sleeping none,
Fitting in with the guys.

I remember
When I was a young soldier in Vietnam,
Shooting gooks and heroin,
Fitting in with the guys.

I remember
Years of jail,
Years of dope and years of hell,
Fitting in with the guys.

My Feelings

Anonymous, *California*

*E*very time I say I'll change,
To you it seems I lie.
But honestly, from the heart,
I swear I really try.
I have this fear
That comes from deep inside
That I'll always be alone
With no one by my side.
So I've gone through life doing things
To get attention on me.
I wish I could be myself
And finally be set free.
I have a lot of love inside
And that's without a doubt.
I wish that I could open up
And let those feelings out.

The Best Christmas Ever

David Hale, *Virginia*

*T*he best Christmas I ever had was last Christmas. I had a good job and I was working hard. I had a lot of good things going for me.

My wife and I were drinking coffee on Christmas morning. Around 6:00 A.M., my son woke up and came running in the living room. "Did Santa Claus come?" he said. "Yes," I replied. He was so excited!

My son started opening his presents. It made me feel good just to watch him open his gifts and see how excited he was.

And now it's Christmas a year later and I am in prison.

The Mind Is a Terrible Thing to Waste

Kevin E. Johnson, *Illinois*

*D*earest Brain Cells,

Life is precious and full of wonderful gifts. You play a major part in my life. I was misled and lowered my dignity by using all kinds of drugs. Because I was inconsiderate of myself, you are gone. I never knew how complicated life would be without you. I never thought not having you would stunt my growth.

I used to laugh at the television commercial that showed an egg in a frying pan with a man's deep, scary voice saying, "This is your brain on drugs." I now cry when the commercial comes on. I understand how John Doe feels, struggling to get the monkey off his back and all strength and faith abandons him.

There's nothing I wouldn't do to regain you. I'll never give up faith, no matter how bad things get. The more you are away from me, the stronger my search gets.

Memories of a Ghost Child

Reginald Lee Walker, *New Mexico*

*T*ime and time again, I fought
    and couldn't win;
        too small to defend myself.
No one knew the ghost.
There could have been others just like me.
Who would believe little old me,
        little young me,
Seeing a real ghost jump from a tree?

I often prayed on my knees
        for the ghost to go his way,
        for me to go my way,
            so there wouldn't be another ghostly day.
So little old me,
        little young me,
Could be free like other kids who loved to play.

I wanted to run;
I wanted to hide.
Where to go and who would know?

Thoughts of telling someone,
    I told no one.
My fears kept the ghost unheard.
Little old me,
    little young me,
    friends with the ghost,
Petrified of saying a word.

Sometimes I would shiver,
    other times quiver,
As my tired eyes cried a river.
Was I wrong to go on allowing the ghost a home,
    ending up sadly alone?
Every time the ghost came,
    the ghost always did the same,
Leaving me in childish shame.

I still wanna tell,
    still should tell
    and send the ghost to jail,
    let the ghost rot in hell.

Something isn't right; I know it.
Something isn't right; I should show it.
But who will listen to little old me,
    little young me,
Starting trouble with the family.

The ghost is bigger than me.
The ghost is stronger, you see,
    and has a hidden personality.
So I cry a little more
    and try a little more
To block the ghost from my door.

Am I to blame?
Memories of the ghost never change.
Will my life ever be the same?

The Flower Garden

Clyde Garr, *Oklahoma*

*A*s I lay in bed one night, I saw how I had wasted my life to drink and the wrong kind of women. I was lonely inside. It felt as if there was a big hole inside my chest. I thought how much I wanted the life that so many of my friends had. Most of them had nice homes, good-looking kids and nice wives. And here I was, 38 years old, and all I could say was, "I used to. . . ."

The next day I called a friend. I told him how I felt. He said, "Yes, you do have an empty spot in your heart. But if you will try, and if you want to, you can fill that empty spot with a flower garden. You have a chance to live two lifetimes in one. You can have the life you deserve." He told me that I must love to be loved—and treat others as I would want to be treated.

I used my friend's advice. And one day I noticed that the empty spot in my chest was not there. I have found a deeper love for my wife, my buddy, my friend than I had known before. I see things today that I never saw before. I recognize fine qualities like beauty, charm, gaiety and the gift of being easy to talk to. In two more days, I will take my G.E.D. test—I began at a fifth-grade level and now I'm getting ready to start college.

I know this, no trumpets sound when the important decisions of our lives are made. Destiny comes quietly when the wheels turn within our hearts. I like to think today that there is a flower garden growing in that empty spot in my chest.

Healing

Anonymous, *California*

When you hurt a lot,
You're sad for a long time,
Not where it shows.
You still smile.
Sometimes your eyes light up
But you breathe more slowly, more deeply.
You look around more.
The streets and the people are not quite real.
Your rooms and your own clothes seem strange
      to you.

People's words hit you funny.
You turn from their meanings.
The words make you hurt inside.

People look at you, their eyes question.
They wonder what they said.
They wonder how soon they can get away from
The feeling of your sadness.

You don't think of being happy again.
You first try not to be sad always.
You keep busy with everyday things
So you won't go mad.

Then, one day,
You hit the sore place.
You catch your breath waiting for the pain,
Waiting for the pain that suddenly isn't there.
Shyly, you poke at it a little.
You want to see how much you can bear.

Little by little, you know
You healed because some people were kind.
They didn't run from your anger.
They reached around your pain.
You healed because in you is a faith
In the rightness of life,
In you is a spirit that holds on.
When flesh is weak,
In you is the habit of keeping on.

For My Son

Mark L. Radmall, *Massachusetts*

This is my fourth time here and I told myself that I would not come back to this place. I don't want you to come here.

Prison is hard time. All you get to do is go to programs and go to recreation, then you go back to your cell. You could read a book or write a letter to your mom or your wife or a friend. Sometimes it's nice to talk to someone in here—a friend or a counselor or even a priest.

Now let's talk about the bad things in here, son. This jail is over 100 years old and the cells are six feet by eight feet. That's not enough room to move around in. The food here is so bad, you feel like throwing up. If you get in a fight, you will go to the "hole" or be "deadlocked." You can't talk back to the correctional officers or you will get written up and given 48 hours in your cell. When I was here before, I got deadlocked for 21 days. I did not talk to anyone at all. It made me crazy.

When I first came here, I was scared like you would be. When you are in here, all you think about is how nice it is outside and all you see is walls and bars. You don't see the trees and the grass and the flowers. You don't get to go swimming. You can't go for a walk with your girlfriend through the woods to see animals. You can't go and feed the ducks at the lake or go horseback riding.

The thing I miss the most is my mom because I can't give her a hug or a kiss. I wish that I never got into this mess.

My Cage

Leonard Young, *California*

Inside of my cage, there is no light.
There is no day and there is no night.
There are only three walls, a ceiling and floor,
Some stainless steel bars that serve as my door.
My amusement consists of what I can find
Inside of my cage or inside of my mind.
Usually there is nothing at all,
Nothing at all except me and this rage,
This burning hate for those who say
That I may be better because of this cage.

Shannon

Christian Carlson, *California*

Did you have a happy birthday, Shannon?
I wasn't there, I wouldn't know.
How was your Christmas this year, Shannon?
I'm sorry I had someplace to go.
And did you color eggs at Easter?
Were you a witch on Halloween?
I'll bet you have some questions too,
Like just where have I been.

Well, I spent a lot of time in jail,
In programs for my addictions.
I never wanted you to share
In your old man's afflictions.
So I spent some time just wandering
The streets of many towns.
I knew that if you saw me,
You'd only be let down.

I guess that what I'm trying to say, and I
         hope you understand,
Is I've always loved you with all my heart,
         no matter where I've been.

47

The Day I Got Married

John Bowles, *Virginia*

It was January. When I first woke up, I was nervous. I looked out the window and it was snowing hard. My fiancée called four or five times, wondering if everything would go as planned. She was worried about the snow.

Before the wedding, the whole family got together at my aunt's house. As we left the house, my aunt slipped on the sidewalk and fell, but she wasn't hurt bad.

At the wedding, everything went okay until we both put the rings on the wrong fingers. My sister-in-law tried to get our attention.

After the ceremony, we were in a hurry to leave the church. Everyone was laughing and joking with us as we went out. My brother accidentally stepped on the train of my wife's dress and tore it and got it all muddy.

During the reception, it really felt funny dancing with my wife since she was pregnant. Her stomach was large and got in the way when we danced.

After the reception, we went to a motel for a few days for our honeymoon. Looking back, even though the marriage didn't work, I wouldn't have done anything differently.

Life in the Barrio

Robert M. Lucero II, *New Mexico*

I grew up on the west side of Albuquerque, New Mexico. My life as a youngster was very thrilling and very scary. I was raised around drug dealers and gang members who didn't care about anyone or anything except money. As I grew up around this environment, I grew into it. Even today, I am still associated with a west side gang, but I am not into gangbanging anymore.

I almost lost my little brother to gangbanging. I have learned that all gangbanging is going to do is bring sorrow to me and my family and other families.

Today, I sit in prison because of my involvement in a gang dispute which ended in murder. I hope to get out of prison soon and get on with my life. I hope that people won't judge me for what I've done, but for what I have become and want to do. Now that I have a family, I am looking to succeed and stay out of prison.

What I See When I Look at a Picture of Myself

Shilo L. Cutler, *Massachusetts*

I see a child, a child who wants the world to notice him—not because he craves attention in life, but because he desperately wants to be remembered after he has gone.

I see a young man, a young man with a sparkle in his eyes. He is happy, happy because he believes in dreams that most people give up on as they grow older. He knows the secret to them.

I see an aging soul when I look past that sparkle. Time and painful events cling to him inside. I can see it in his eyes. Those damned eyes. I hate to look at those eyes.

I can see life, life as all life grows. I see nothing new or unusual, just life and a young man in a picture that someone took so they could look at it later on and remember him the way he was after he is gone.

I Praise God

Felix Ilert, *New York*

When I was on the outside,
I didn't know the Lord.
But I have found him inside prison.
I feel safe
Knowing the Lord won't let me down.
On the outside,
I was a mess.
I didn't care about myself.
But now I am in prison
Locked in a cage.
Alone.
I'm filled with rage.
No one to turn to
Or to call a friend.
But I don't sweat
Nor shed a tear.
For, in my heart,
I have someone with me at all times,
Someone I can call a friend.
That's why
I praise God.

Shining Star

Anonymous, *California*

As I look out my window,
Everything is so unbelievably beautiful.
The still of the night
Brings peace of mind to one's soul.

I gaze through my window.
    A shining star
    Stands out among
    Many stars—
    Shining down
    On my face
    As if to let me know
    On a lonely night,
    I am still
    Not all
    alone.

Letter to the Editor

Anonymous, *California*

*F*rom the many years I have spent incarcerated, I know that there are limited opportunities for finding the help necessary for convicts to change. Most incarcerated people are doing time because of drug-related cases. Because of the lack of programs, most prisons and county jails remain negative environments where, on a regular basis, people fantasize and plot to get high.

Prisons have become places to warehouse people. Billions of dollars have been spent on prisons in an attempt to reduce crime. Obviously, the attempt has failed because crime has exploded. The money spent to house criminals has been taken from necessary social programs such as education, health care and social services.

Looking into the problem, I have discovered that lack of education is a major factor in the growth of crime. Instead of increasing the number of prisons, the government should develop educational programs both in and out of prison. This would offer both inmates and parolees the opportunity to become productive people in society. Recovery should be the objective, thus breaking the chains of recidivism. Addicted convicts, such as myself, would appreciate the opportunity to become part of the solution and help eliminate the problem. We realize the solution lies in learning a new, restructured and educated life.

I have been in and out of jails for most of my life. This program is what I need and want. I hope that our society will see what a difference is being made, not only with myself but with other inmates. We are serious about recovery.

The Art of Deer Hunting

Timothy F. Buck, *Massachusetts*

*D*eer hunting is an exciting sport. Like any sport, you have to work hard and practice. You can't just jump into it and expect results. It takes a lot of time and patience to become a good deer hunter.

Before you start, you have to get your equipment. There are two legal ways to hunt deer. One is with a shotgun and the other is with a bow and arrow (or archery). Each has its own season. Archery is first in early November; shotgun comes later.

After choosing your weapon, the next thing is to find a place to hunt. This is a tricky task. Deer are in the woods, but where? You can find out where by talking to other hunters or reading hunting magazines.

After doing your research, you must scout the area where you think or know deer are. Walk through the woods, look around for marks. Deer leave tracks. They also leave other marks—scrapes on the ground, shredded saplings where bucks have rubbed their antlers, depressed places where deer have bedded down and many more. After you have done more hunting and reading, you will recognize these marks easier.

After you have found a spot where you think deer will be, you can hunt. Make sure all your equipment is in order and, most importantly, make sure you have a hunting license. You are ready to do what you have worked so hard for. Good luck!

Refresher Course

Anonymous, *California*

I remember
The taste of freedom,
Making my own choices,
No one telling me what to do or when to do it.

I remember
What real food tastes like,
The smell of it cooking,
The creativity of having planned it.

I remember
Being alone,
Listening to music
Or sitting on a hillside.

I remember
Driving a car,
Wanting to go somewhere,
Having the freedom to do it.

I remember
Seeing friends,
Being together
Comfortable in each other's company.

I remember
My cat,
A stupid ball of fur,
One of my best friends.

I remember
What it's like to spend money
On something I want or need,
And especially for someone else.

I remember
Going out for a meal,
Sharing it with someone,
Trying something new.

I remember
Just hanging out,
Doing what I want to do
Or maybe what we want to do.

I remember
What it's like to be free.
But I'm starting to forget.
I need a refresher course.

Divorce

Willie Glover, *Virginia*

Divorce is a depressing thought, be it in prison or as a free person. It means the same thing: you are losing someone you love. Just recently, I received a letter from my wife telling me of her desire for a divorce. What can you say? What can you do? Very little, actually. Just accept the decision of your loved one—and learn to cope. I had difficulty answering my wife's letter, for I still care for her. Yet I want her to be happy.

Being incarcerated certainly hurt my marriage. Perhaps it was the final nail in the coffin. Marriage is a full-time job, requiring two working as one, with no holidays. My wife is a good person, but being separated took its toll on both of us. In a way, she's in a prison minus the bars and fences.

Love is just a word, but try living without it. Try to do anything without the most wonderful of all gifts—the love of a man and a woman. Yes, writing to a loved one who is no longer a loved one is difficult—just like life itself. Enjoy life and love—they're precious. And too soon, they can be taken away.

Oceanfront Memories

Larry Daniel, *Virginia*

I used to live near the beach. I owned my own company. I miss the hard work, meeting new people and, of course, making money. But the oceanfront is what I miss most.

My son and I enjoyed fishing. Our catch usually included one of my favorites, flounder. Afterwards, we walked along the boardwalk, scoping out the lovely ladies. We searched for a nice open area where I could lie back and enjoy the sun's warm rays while my boy built sandcastles. The water was usually pretty cold, but we got used to it after a couple of dips. Sometimes we took along a Frisbee to throw around and bread crumbs to feed the sea gulls. We loved watching them hover and swoop through the air.

The beach is especially nice at night. There's a certain serenity that helps one relax. I would walk through the shallow tides, listening to the waves roll to the shore. The moonlight shone on the water. There always seemed to be a nice cool breeze. Go to the beach and you will see how the oceanfront will set you free.

Where is the Hope?

Anonymous, *Illinois*

Where is the hope? Is there hope in our future? Many of you probably feel as I do. We need to rewind the tape and see where we went wrong.

Where is the hope? I have news for you, brother. The hope is here in this room. We have to start somewhere. Why not start with ourselves? We are in jail, true, but we don't have to give up the hope.

We have the key to living a good life. Education is the key. Education is the beginning of our future. The past is gone. If we don't take advantage of this opportunity, we could be lost forever.

Clyde says that every day in here is wasted. But if you get an education here, the days aren't wasted.

So, where is the hope? It is here in my hands. It is here in your hands. It is here in our hands. That is where the hope is.

To Our Readers

We hope to publish more anthologies like this one. But to do that, we need writing by you, our readers. If you are enrolled in an adult basic-skills program or an ESOL program, we would like to see your writing. If you have a piece of writing you would like us to consider for a future book, please send it to us. It can be on any subject; it can be a true story, a play, fiction or poetry. We can't promise that we will publish your story, but we will give it serious consideration. We will let you know what our decision is.

Please do not send us your original manuscript. Instead, make a copy of it and send that to us, because we can't promise that we will be able to return it to you.

If you send us your writing, we will assume you are willing for us to publish it. If we decide to accept it, we will send a letter requesting your permission. So please be sure to include your name, address and phone number on the copy you send us.

We look forward to seeing your writing.

The Editors
Readers House
Literacy Volunteers of New York City
121 Avenue of the Americas, New York, NY 10013

Four series of good books for all readers:

Writers' Voices—A multicultural, whole-language series of books offering selections from some of America's finest writers, along with background information, maps, glossaries, questions and activities and many more supplementary materials. Our list of authors includes: Amy Tan * Alex Haley * Alice Walker * Rudolfo Anaya * Louise Erdrich * Oscar Hijuelos * Maxine Hong Kingston * Gloria Naylor * Anne Tyler * Tom Wolfe * Mario Puzo * Avery Corman * Judith Krantz * Larry McMurtry * Mary Higgins Clark * Stephen King * Peter Benchley * Ray Bradbury * Sidney Sheldon * Maya Angelou * Jane Goodall * Mark Mathabane * Loretta Lynn * Katherine Jackson * Carol Burnett * Kareem Abdul-Jabbar * Ted Williams * Ahmad Rashad * Abigail Van Buren * Priscilla Presley * Paul Monette * Robert Fulghum * Bill Cosby * Lucille Clifton * Robert Bly * Robert Frost * Nikki Giovanni * Langston Hughes * Joy Harjo * Edna St. Vincent Millay * William Carlos Williams * Terrence McNally * Jules Feiffer * Alfred Uhry * Horton Foote * Marsha Norman * Lynne Alvarez * Lonne Elder III * ntozake shange * Neil Simon * August Wilson * Harvey Fierstein * Beth Henley * David Mamet * Arthur Miller and Spike Lee.

New Writers' Voices—A series of anthologies and individual narratives by talented new writers. Stories, poems and true-life experiences written by adult learners cover such topics as health, home and family, love, work, facing challenges, being in prison and remembering life in native countries. Many *New Writers' Voices* books contain photographs or illustrations.

Reference—A reference library for adult new readers and writers.

OurWorld—A series offering selections from works by well-known science writers, including David Attenborough, Thor Heyerdahl and Carl Sagan. Books include photographs, illustrations, related articles.

Write for our free complete catalog: Readers House/LVNYC, 121 Avenue of the Americas, New York, NY 10013